D084895ろ

FLEAS
Feasting on Blood

BARBARA A. SOMERVILL

PowerKiDS press™

New York

Published in 2008 by The Rosen Publishing Group, Inc.
29 East 21st Street, New York, NY 10010

First Edition

Editor: Joanne Randolph
Book Design: Dean Galiano
Layout Design: Greg Tucker
Photo Researcher: Nicole Pristash

Photo Credits: Cover © David Scharf/Getty Images; pp. 5, 11, 15, 17, 19 Shutterstock.com; p. 7 © www.istockphoto.com/Daniel Mathys; p. 9 © www.istockphoto.com/Charity Myers; p. 13 © G. I. Bernard/OSF/Animals Animals; p. 21 © George Bernard/Animals Animals.

Library of Congress Cataloging-in-Publication Data

Somervill, Barbara A.
   Fleas : feasting on blood / Barbara A. Somervill. — 1st ed.
      p. cm. — (Bloodsuckers)
   Includes index.
   ISBN-13: 978-1-4042-3805-3 (library binding)
   ISBN-10: 1-4042-3805-0 (library binding)
   1. Fleas—Juvenile literature. I. Title.
   QL599.5.S66 2007
   595.77'5—dc22
                                                2006103426

Manufactured in the United States of America

CONTENTS

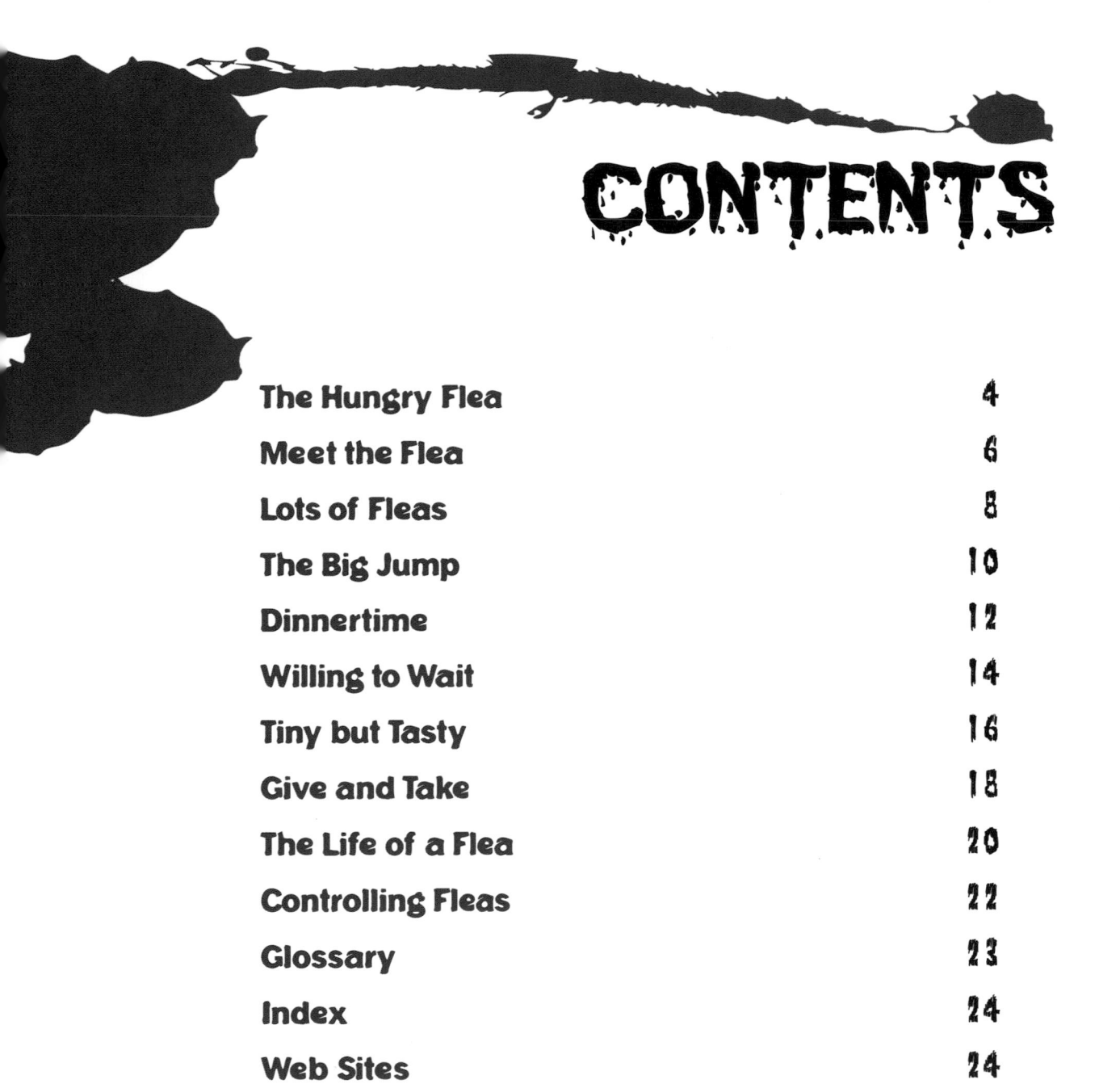

THE HUNGRY FLEA

A family moves into a house, and within a week everyone has bites on their lower legs. The bites are from fleas. Do not always blame the dog, though! It is likely that the flea eggs and **larvae** were in the rug when the other owners moved out.

Ten adult female fleas and their offspring can produce 250,000 fleas in 30 days. The fleas in the house will be in different forms. There will be eggs, larvae, **pupae**, and adults. Adults stay in pupal cases until food arrives. When the family moved in, the hungry fleas were ready for a feast.

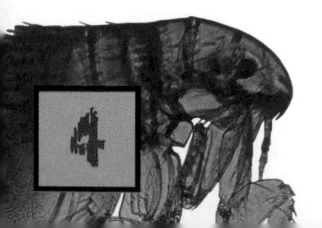

Cats and dogs may bring fleas into a house. Once the fleas come in, their eggs and pupal cases can lay waiting for months for food.

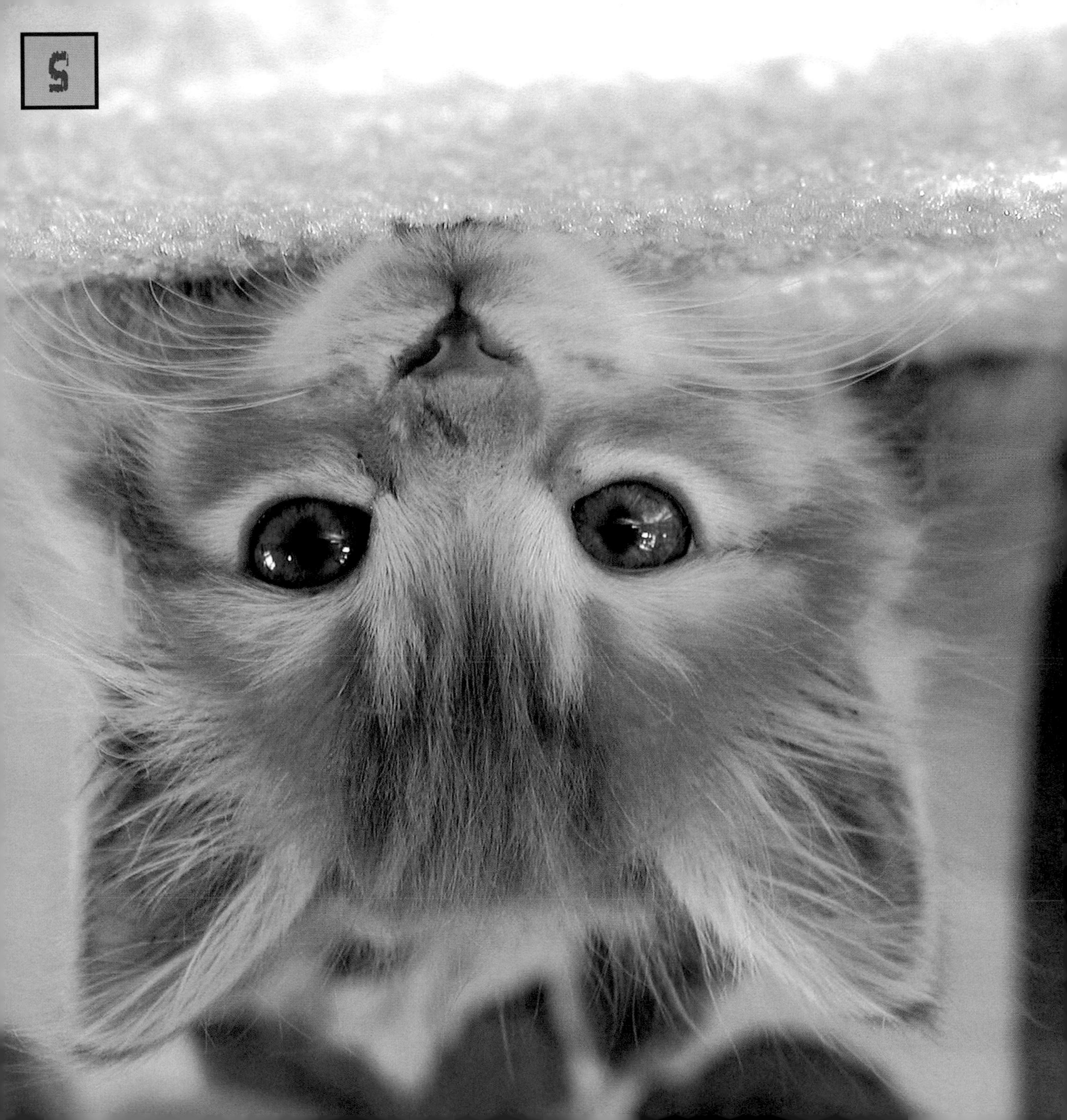

MEET THE FLEA

Fleas are small, wingless **insects** that are usually reddish-brown in color. Their body measures from ⅟₁₆ to ⅛ inch (2–3 mm) long and is covered with a hard outer shell, called an **exoskeleton**. The flea's body is flat on the sides to allow it to crawl through hair.

A flea's head is small, with sharp **mandibles** for biting. Fleas also have a **proboscis**, which is like a straw for sucking blood.

Like other insects, fleas have six legs with many hairs. Claws at the end of each leg allow the flea to hold on to **prey**.

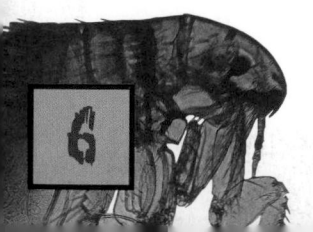

Fleas' eyes are very small and see only bright light. This close-up shot of a flea was taken with a special tool called a scanning electron microscope.

LOTS OF FLEAS

There are about 250 kinds of fleas in North America and many more **species** around the world. Fleas can be sorted into three basic groups. These groups are mobile, **sedentary**, and sticktight.

Mobile fleas change **hosts** often. They spend time in nests, bedding, or on the host. Sedentary fleas like to stay in one place. Sticktight fleas do just what their name says. The females dig into an animal's skin and hold tight. They mate and lay eggs from this place. The female then dies inside the animal's skin, and her body causes sickness.

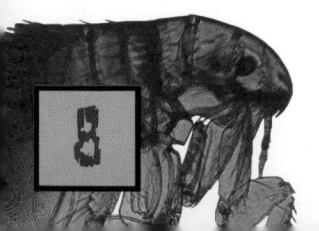

Flea bites can make an animal itch, or have an uneasy feeling on its skin. This dog is scratching to make the itch feel better.

THE BIG JUMP

The most shocking thing about fleas is their ability to jump. Fleas have six legs, but the back pair of legs is very long and strong. This long, strong set of legs allows a flea to jump 14 to 16 inches (36–41 cm). This is quite a jump for an animal as small as a flea.

Fleas can jump up to 200 times their body length and 130 times their height. Fleas make such jumps many times each day. This would be like a person jumping over the U.S. Capitol building 200 times in one day.

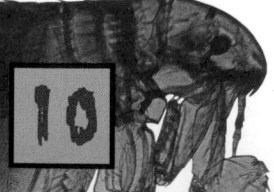
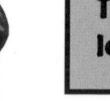

This is a magnified, or blown-up, photo of a flea. The fleas' back legs are very long and strong.

10

DINNERTIME

Fleas drink blood, but they do so only as adults. As larvae, the fleas feed on the **feces** of other fleas, dry skin, and small insects, such as mites. Once they are adults, fleas must have a blood meal or they will die.

To drink, fleas cut into the skin of their prey with their sharp mandibles. They then put something into the bite that keeps the blood flowing while they eat. Females need a blood meal to be able to lay their eggs.

This flea is feeding on a rabbit's ear. Do you see how it has fixed itself to the animal to suck its blood?

WILLING TO WAIT

Fleas do not so much hunt as lie in wait. When the pupa has changed into an adult flea, the adult does not leave the pupal case right away. It waits for an animal to pass by.

Inside the pupal case, the flea feels the movements of nearby animals or people. If a person or animal steps on the pupal case, this also tells the flea that food is there. Living things give off heat from their body and carbon dioxide from their breath. Fleas know that heat and carbon dioxide equal food.

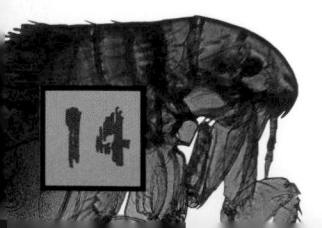

14

When a flea knows that food is near, it springs onto the prey, climbs into a safe place, and bites. This squirrel will make a good lunch for some fleas.

TINY BUT TASTY

Fleas are blood-sucking **parasites**, but they are also prey. Ants and beetles feed on fleas and flea larvae. They attack fleas in nests and holes in the ground. Nematodes, or tiny round worms, feed on fleas, too.

Most large animals cannot rid themselves of fleas, but they have friends who will help them out. Baboons and monkeys pick fleas off one another and eat the fleas they catch. Giraffes, zebras, antelopes, and other large African mammals get help from oxpeckers and other insect-eating birds.

These baboons are grooming each other. They pick through each other's hair to find tasty bugs, like fleas.

GIVE AND TAKE

Fleas do not just take blood from their hosts. They can also give their hosts diseases, or illnesses. It is believed that 30 different species of fleas pass along diseases. The flea bites a sick animal or human and takes in the blood. When the flea bites again, it passes the disease to another animal or human.

The deadliest disease tied to fleas is bubonic plague, also called the black plague. More than one-third of Europe's population died from the plague in the 1300s. Fleas also spread typhus and tapeworms.

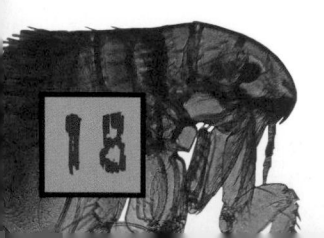

It is thought that rats carried the bubonic plague, and the fleas that fed on the rats gave the plague to humans.

19

THE LIFE OF A FLEA

In a place infested by fleas, about 50 **percent** of the fleas are eggs, 35 percent are larvae, 10 percent are pupae, and 5 percent are adults. Females can lay up to 50 eggs a day. The tiny, white eggs fall onto rugs, bedding, and soil. After 1 to 10 days, tiny worms, the larvae, leave the eggs.

The larvae wiggle into spaces in the floor or into rugs. They feed and grow until they are ready to change form again. They spin sticky silk pupal cases. The adults form inside the pupal cases, waiting for a meal to come along.

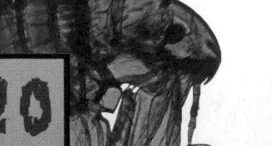

This flea pupal case lies waiting in a rug. The whole life cycle of a flea takes from two weeks to a full year.

CONTROLLING FLEAS

Fleas have lived on Earth for millions of years and will likely continue to live for many more. There are flea species that feed on just about every animal. Many species are named for the animals they most like, such as cat fleas, dog fleas, and rat fleas.

Fleas are hard to control, but many products can help. Flea shampoos, **collars**, or **medicine** can be used to control fleas on pets. Natural flea controls can be used, too. Fleas dislike citronella candles, eucalyptus oil, balsam, and yucca. Even with all these products, though, fleas are probably here to stay.

GLOSSARY

collars (KAH-lerz) Thin bands worn around the neck.

exoskeleton (ek-soh-SKEH-leh-tun) The hard covering on the outside of an animal's body that holds and guards the soft insides.

feces (FEE-seez) The solid waste of animals.

hosts (HOHSTS) Animals that are food for another animal but that do not die and do not get anything in return.

insects (IN-sekts) Small animals that often have six legs and wings.

larvae (LAHR-vee) Animals in the early life period in which they have a wormlike form.

mandibles (MAN-dih-bulz) The paired mouthparts of an insect that generally move side to side.

medicine (MEH-duh-sin) A drug that a doctor gives you to help fight illness.

parasites (PER-uh-syts) Living things that live in, on, or with another living thing.

percent (pur-SENT) One part of 100.

prey (PRAY) An animal that is hunted by another animal for food.

proboscis (pruh-BAH-sus) A tubelike mouthpart that insects use to suck in liquid food.

pupae (PYOO-pee) The second period of life for an insect, in which it changes from a larva to an adult.

sedentary (SEH-den-ter-ee) Staying in the same place.

species (SPEE-sheez) One kind of living thing. All people are one species.

INDEX

C
collars, 22

E
eggs, 4, 8, 12, 20
exoskeleton, 6

F
feces, 12

G
groups, 8

H
host(s), 8, 18

I
insects, 6, 12

L
larvae, 4, 12, 16, 20

M
mandibles, 6, 12
medicine, 22

P
parasites, 16
prey, 6, 16
proboscis, 6
pupa(e), 4, 14, 20

S
species, 8, 22

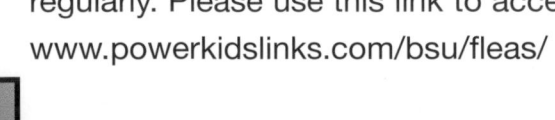

WEB SITES

Due to the changing nature of Internet links, PowerKids Press has developed an online list of Web sites related to the subject of this book. This site is updated regularly. Please use this link to access the list:
www.powerkidslinks.com/bsu/fleas/